BRITAIN SINCE WORLD WAR II

Media and Entertainment

COLIN HYNSON

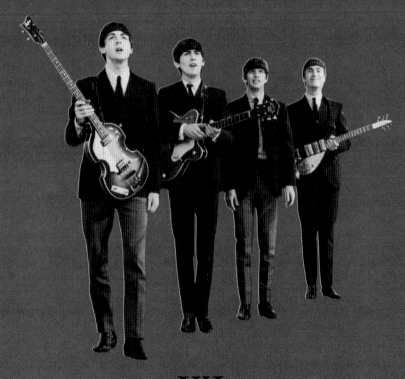

W

FRANKLIN WATTS
LONDON·SYDNEY

First published in 2007 by
Franklin Watts
338 Euston Road
London NW1 3BH

Franklin Watts Australia
Level 17/207 Kent Street
Sydney NSW 2000
Copyright © Franklin Watts 2007

Editor: Jeremy Smith
Art director: Jonathan Hair
Design: Jason Anscomb
Picture researcher: Sophie Hartley

A CIP catalogue record for this book
is available from the British Library.

Picture credits: Andrew Linscott/Alamy: 11. David
Parker/Science Photo Library: 16b. David
Levenson/Alamy: 9. Getty images: 8t, 10l, 18t, 20t, 22.
Ian Miles - Flashpoint Pictures/Alamy: 15. John
Rogers/Rex Features: 27b. John Sturrock/Alamy: 25t.
Mary Evans/Juliette Soester 23b. Novastock/Rex
Features: 7. Novastock/Rex Features: 14. PCL/Alamy:
13b. Peter Brooker/Rex Features: 27t. Photofusion
Picture Library/Alamy: 21. Popperfoto.com: 8b, 16t, 20b,
26. PYMCA/Alamy: 24. Topfoto: 6t. Time: 6b.

Dewey Classification: 941.085

ISBN: 978 0 7496 7609 4

Printed in China

Franklin Watts is a division of Hachette Children's Books,
an Hachette Livre UK company.

CONTENTS

Since World War II the British people have twice come together to celebrate, learn and to be entertained. In 1951, the "Festival of Britain" took place on the South Bank in London. Nearly 50 years later, the Millennium Dome was created in Greenwich to celebrate the year 2000. During the time between these celebrations, the way people in Britain chose to spend their leisure time and the technology available to them changed almost beyond recognition.

▲ Crowds sitting at an outdoor café during the Festival of Britain on May 5th, 1951.

THE FESTIVAL OF BRITAIN

In 1948, the Labour government decided that the British people needed a celebration to lift their spirits after the difficulties of the war years. The "Festival of Britain" was meant to show people a new and better life on offer to everybody. Under the leadership of Herbert Morrison, the "Festival of Britain" opened in May 1951, and remained open until November. It was made up of a series of buildings including the "Dome of Discovery", "Land of Britain" and "Sea and Ships".

There was also a giant cigar-shaped sculpture called the "Skylon". The festival was seen as a great success and actually made a small profit.

▶ A portrait of Herbert Morrison, the Labour politician behind the "Festival of Britain".

> " *I travelled to London on a coach from my small grammar school in Gloucestershire, and most of the other girls had never been to London before. We travelled on the tube, which some of them found frightening. We visited the South Bank site, and were impressed by the Dome of Discovery. I bought a souvenir book to show my family, and a Festival of Britain biro.* "
>
> **Janet Johnson remembers visiting the Festival of Britain.**

THE MILLENNIUM DOME

It was in 1994 that the idea for a second dome to celebrate the coming of a new millennium was first discussed by the British government. In 1997, under the Labour Prime Minister Tony Blair, the idea was picked up and expanded. A member of Parliament called Peter Mandelson was put in charge of the running of the Dome. It opened to the public on 1st January 2000. The Dome was divided into 14 "zones" such as the "Body", "Learning" and "Money" zone. From the start the Dome was controversial, and it was seen by many as a failure. It did not attract the visitors it expected and the government had to ask for money from the National Lottery on several occasions to keep it going. The Dome is now called "The O2".

BRITAIN BETWEEN THE CELEBRATIONS

Since the "Festival of Britain", the way Britons chose to live their lives, and in particular the ways in which they could spend their leisure time, changed beyond recognition. In 1948, people listened to the radio to stay up to date with the news, or occasionally visited the theatre or cinema. Gramophones were the preserve of the rich. Today, most of us own televisions – often with satellite channels – and we have dozens of radio stations to listen to, as well as being able to listen to pop music on CD or download music from the Internet onto MP3 players. There is also a far greater choice of newspapers to read, plus games consoles that make the earliest computers look positively primitive.

The number of people who visited the Festival of Britain was 6 million. 6.5 million people visited the Millennium Dome. However, the Dome was open throughout the whole of 2000 whereas the Festival of Britain was only open between May and November 1951.

◀ The Millennium Dome lit up at night by changing colour displays.

TIMELINE

1948
The Labour government decides to host the "Festival of Britain".

1951
The "Festival of Britain" opens on the South Bank in May.

1994
Prime Minister John Major comes up with the idea of the Millennium Dome.

2000
The Dome opens to the public on 1st January and closes on 31st December.

2005
The Dome was sold to the company O2 who reopen it as a sports and entertainment venue.

BUZZ BOX

One of the most interesting links between the Festival of Britain and the Millennium Dome is between the two people who were in charge of both occasions. Both Herbert Morrison and Peter Mandelson were MPs, and Mandelson is Morrison's grandson.

In the years before World War II, listening to the radio was the main form of news and entertainment. Most homes had only one radio which all of the family would listen to. Today most homes have more than one radio, and there are dozens of national and local stations to choose from.

ONLY FOUR STATIONS

At the end of World War II, British people had a choice of just four radio stations, and three of those were run by the BBC. The three BBC stations were the "Light Programme" which broadcast entertainment and music, the "Third Programme" which broadcast plays and classical music and the "Home Service" which transmitted light music and talks. Their only competitor was "Radio Luxembourg". This station had a club and radio show for children called the "Ovaltineys".

THE RISE OF THE PIRATES

At the start of the 1960s, many people (particularly young people) began to feel that the BBC radio stations were too formal and didn't play the kind of music that they wanted to listen to. To fill this gap,

A gale force wind was blowing in the North Sea off the east coast of England one night during the winter of 1966… The boat was rockin' in more ways than one as I turned up the monitor speakers … to drown out the sound of the storm that was raging outside.

Steve Young, a DJ on the pirate radio station "Radio Caroline".

pirate radio stations began to appear between 1964 and 1967. They were called pirate stations because they were based on ships just off the British coast and operated outside the law. The most famous "pirates" were "Radio Caroline" and "Wonderful Radio London". In 1967, the BBC scrapped their old stations and launched Radio 1, 2, 3 and 4.

▶ Radio 1 and 2 DJs and presenters shown in 1968.

BUZZ BOX

The first DJ (disc jockey) on Radio 1 was Tony Blackburn, and his first words were: "And, good morning everyone. Welcome to the exciting new sound of Radio 1." Since then Radio 1 has had many famous DJs such as John Peel, Chris Moyles, Judge Jules and Pete Tong.

GREATER CHOICE

In 1973, the first British commercial radio stations were launched. These were "LBC" (a talk station) and "Capital Radio" (a music station). It was not until after 1992 that more radio stations began to broadcast. "Classic FM" was the first national commercial radio station and this was soon followed by other stations such as "Virgin Radio". The arrival of digital radio created new stations that catered for particular musical tastes. For instance, "Jazz FM" plays jazz music and "Kerrang! Radio" plays heavy metal. There are also stations for Britain's ethnic minorities, such as "London Greek Radio" and "Asian Plus".

▲ "Radio Caroline", the pirate radio pop station moored off the Isle of Man, pictured in 1966.

◄ DJ Pirate Bams from the independent "Kiss FM" radio station.

TIMELINE

1945
The "Home Service" and "Light Programme" stations starts broadcasting.

1946
The "Third Programme" starts broadcasting.

1964
The first pirate station, "Radio Caroline", starts broadcasting.

1967
The BBC launches Radio 1, 2, 3 and 4.

1973
The first commercial stations are launched in London.

1992
"Classic FM" is Britain's first national commercial station.

THEN AND NOW

While there were only four stations to listen to in 1945, there are now 30 national radio stations. There are also about 200 local and digital radio stations.

The 1940s and early 1950s were the years when going to the cinema was one of the most popular forms of entertainment for British people. The number of people who went to the cinema during World War II actually went up. This was partly because people looked for a distraction from wartime Britain and also because cinemas played newsreels that kept people up to date with the latest events in the war..

▲ Julie Andrews in *The Sound of Music*, 1965.

THE DECLINE BEGINS

At the start of the 1950s, going to the cinema was still a very popular activity for many British people. In 1951, over one billion cinema tickets were sold in Britain. Many families went to the cinema at least once a week. There would normally be two films shown along with cartoons. After that year, cinema attendance began to fall. One of the main reasons for this was the arrival of television. When ITV started in 1955, they began to show films on Saturday afternoons and people stayed at home to watch films.

GETTING SMALLER

By 1984, cinema attendance had fallen to just 54 million. This was just one visit a year for every man, woman and child in Britain.

> ❝ *I loved going to the pictures. The programme changed four times a week and the excitement began by looking through the big glass window and seeing photographs of the films and deciding which one was best. We had to set off early to join the long queue: first stop was the sweet shop where, with two pence to spend, I chose from my favourites - gobstoppers, aniseed balls, puff candy, black jacks or black bullets.* ❞

Linda Kenyon remembering going to the cinema in the 1960s.

BUZZ BOX

Britain's biggest cinema is Star City near Birmingham. It was opened in 1996. It has 30 screens and can seat over 4,000 people. It regularly shows "Bollywood" films that appeal to the local Asian communities.

▲ A multiplex cinema in Newcastle.

People did not like sitting in large, almost empty cinemas and the arrival of video recorders meant that people could watch even more films at home. Things began to improve in 1985 with the arrival of the multiplex cinema. These were cinemas with several small screens all showing different films. The first multiplex in Britain was opened in Milton Keynes in 1985. Now most large towns have multiplex cinemas.

GOING BACK TO THE CINEMA

After 1985, people started to return to the cinema. In 1994, over 124 million cinema tickets were sold in Britain. People liked the new multiplex cinemas that were often built along with other kinds of entertainment nearby, such as restaurants and bowling alleys. This meant that people could enjoy several leisure activities in one place.

▲ A family buy popcorn at Zeffirellis cinema in Ambleside, Cumbria.

THEN AND NOW

In 1945, just over 1.5 billion cinema tickets were sold in Britain. In 2003, that figure was about 167 million. That means that today everybody on average is going to the cinema about three times a year.

TIMELINE

1946
The peak of cinema going, with over 1.5 billion attendances in a year.

1955
The arrival of commercial television starts a decline in cinema attendance.

1984
Cinema attendance is just 54 million – the lowest since World War II.

1985
The first multiplex is built in Milton Keynes.

1996
"Star City" – Britain's biggest cinema – is built near Birmingham.

It was only in 1932 that regular television broadcasting started in Britain when the BBC started to transmit programmes to just a few thousand people in the London area. All television was stopped on the day that World War II (1939-1945) started and did not begin again until June 1946.

TELEVISION BECOMES POPULAR

Even after television broadcasting started again very few homes could actually receive the programmes and even fewer actually had a television. However, in June 1953, the BBC was given permission to televise the crowning of the new Queen Elizabeth II from inside Westminster Abbey. This event encouraged many more people to buy a television. In 1955, a new commercial television service run by ITV began in Britain. This new channel also encouraged people to buy a television for their home.

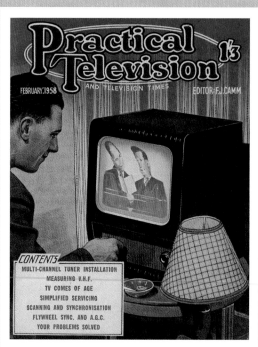

▲ An 1950s advertisment for an early television set.

MANY MORE CHANNELS

Until the 1990s, people had the choice of only four television stations: two from the BBC, one from ITV, and Channel 4 (which launched in 1982). In 1990, BSkyB (now called Sky) started to transmit television programmes which, so long as people bought the right kind of satellite dish, brought many more channels into people's homes. The arrival of digital television in 1998 and the launch of Freeview in 2002 meant that there are now over 150 television channels to choose from.

◄ Satellite dishes line a street in North Devon.

GOOD OR BAD?

There has been a lot of debate about whether television has had a good or bad influence on modern Britain. It has certainly allowed everybody to learn much more about the world that they live in and has given us all a huge choice of entertainment shows such as "Big Brother" and "Neighbours".

However, many people have worried about the amount of television that some people watch (about 2 hours per day) and there has also been some concern about the bad influence that television has on young people. The children's programme "Grange Hill" started in 1978, and was often attacked for some of its "realistic" stories.

BUZZ BOX

When BBC Television stopped broadcasting on 1st September 1939, the last programme shown was a Disney cartoon – *Mickey's Gala Premiere*. When television started again on 6th June 1946, the first programme they showed was exactly the same cartoon.

▲ A 12-year-old girl watches television in her bedroom. Some people think children and teenagers watch much too much television.

THEN AND NOW

In 1954, just over three million homes in Britain had a television, about one in three homes. In 2007, over 25 million homes had at least one television and only about 500,000 homes had no television. Television now plays a major part in the free time of most people in Britain today.

GOING TO THE THEATRE

For hundreds of years British people have been entertained by a visit to the theatre. There have been fears that with the rise of the cinema and television people would stop going to the theatre to see plays. However, since World War II, theatre-going has become more and more popular.

THE "WEST END"

After World War II, the "West End" of London remained the centre of British theatre. Most of the plays that are performed there are "commercial". That means that they do not rely on government money and any plays that they perform have to make a profit. The most popular kinds of plays are comedies, who-dunnits like *The Mousetrap* and musicals like *Cats*, *The Lion King* or *Les Miserables*.

> **"***My husband was manager of a busy general printers, and an important contract was for the printing of London theatre programmes. For the first time in our lives we found ourselves in the posh seats. Halcyon days, particularly with plays at the Royal Court, introducing us to Wesker, and to Pinter, to Osborne and to Beckett … but it wasn't all serious stuff.***"**
>
> Dorien Brooks, a regular theatre-goer, recalls going to the theatre during the 1950s and 1960s.

THEATRES FOR THE NATION

There were demands for a national theatre for many years before World War II. It was only in 1963, however, that the National Theatre was founded. It moved to its current home on London's South Bank in 1976. The Royal Shakespeare Company was created in 1960 with theatres in London and Stratford-upon-Avon (Shakespeare's birthplace) to satisfy the same demand.

◄ A musical from London's West End.

THEN AND NOW

In 1987 about 23% of British people said that they had been to a play during the past year. In 2003 that figure had risen very slightly to 24%.

▲ The National Theatre in London, England.

In 2004, the National Theatre of Scotland (NTS) was created. The NTS today commissions existing theatres and theatre companies, or brings together directors, writers, designers and performers in new combinations to create productions that will play in theatres and other venues up and down Scotland.

ON THE FRINGE

"Fringe" theatre are plays that are performed in small theatres and often look at difficult subjects. After World War II, British fringe theatre grew when a London theatre called the Royal Court showed a play called *Look Back in Anger*. It started a new kind of play called "kitchen-sink" drama, so called because most of the plays were set in ordinary people's houses.

◀ A performance of the play *Look Back in Anger* at the John Osborne Lyric Theatre.

For many years after World War II newspapers were the main source of news and information for many people. Nearly all of the national daily newspapers were based in Fleet Street in London. Today newspapers have moved out of Fleet Street and responded to competition from television and the Internet.

NEWSPAPERS AFTER THE WAR

Most of the national newspapers that are read today were first printed many years before. *The Times* started in 1785 and the *Daily Telegraph* in 1855. The *Daily Mirror* was first produced in 1903 and the *Daily Express* began in 1900. Since the end of World War II only three current national newspapers have started. The *Sun* started in 1964, the *Daily Star* began in 1978 and the *Independent* arrived in 1986. Many of our Sunday newspapers also started after World War II.

CHANGES IN NEWSPAPERS

Newspapers have changed over the past few years as people have begun using the Internet and television for their news and entertainment. The smaller "tabloid" newspapers like the *Sun* and the *Daily Mirror* began reporting news about celebrities and television programmes. After 1986 national newspapers began to move out of Fleet Street and used new technologies to print their newspapers. This started when the *Sun*, *The Times* and the *News of the World* moved to Wapping in East London. Because many people now get their news from the Internet, many large cities now have free newspapers paid for by advertising.

◀ The latest editions come off the press at the *Daily Express* building in Fleet Street during the 1950s.

BUZZ BOX

There are currently 10 major national newspapers. However, they are owned by a smaller number of companies. News International owns two daily newspapers and one free newspaper. Express newspapers own two daily newspapers. There is some concern about companies owning too many newspapers.

CHILDRENS' NEWSPAPERS

There have been attempts to start newspapers just for children. At the end of World War II the *Children's Newspaper* was read by nearly 500,000 children every week. It stopped production in 1965 mostly because of the rise of new children's comics and magazines. In May 2006 a new weekly paper called *First News* was launched. It is aimed at 7-14 year olds and presents news and entertainment stories.

> **❝*I remember that I used to read the* Children's Newspaper *when I was on the Tube (London Underground). I used to feel really grown-up having my own paper and I'd hold up the paper so that everybody could see I was reading it.*❞**
>
> **Memory from the author's mother.**

▲ A famous headline from the *Sun* newspaper, commentating on the fate of the Conservative Party.

THEN AND NOW

In the past few years the number of people reading newspapers has been going down. Only 50% of adults read a daily newspaper. In the past twenty years only the *Daily Mail* and the *Daily Telegraph* have been getting more readers.

► A man handing out copies of the free *London Lite* newspaper.

TIMELINE

1959
The *Manchester Guardian* becomes the *Guardian*.

1964
The *Sun* newspaper starts as a replacement for the *Daily Herald*.

1965
The *Children's Newspaper* stops printing.

1978
The *Daily Star* is launched.

1986
The *Independent* is launched.

The *Sun*, *The Times* and *News of the World* move from Fleet Street to Wapping.

2004
Free newspapers begin to appear in British cities.

TALKING ON THE PHONE

The rise of the telephone has revolutionised the way that we communicate with each other. Telephones have been available in Britain since 1878. However, very few people had a telephone because they were too expensive and that meant that there were not that many people to actually call. It was only from the 1960s that telephones became a normal part of people's lives.

In 1946 there were just under 500,000 work and home telephones in Britain. Today, not including mobile telephones, there are over 35 million telephones in our homes, offices and schools. If mobile phones are included then there are about 90 million phones in Britain today.

TELEPHONES AFTER THE WAR

At the end of World War II the General Post Office (GPO) was the only provider of telephones in Britain. At the time the Labour government was nationalising many of Britain's major industries. In 1947, the GPO was brought under the control of the British government. Not only did the GPO control all of the telephone lines but it was also the only legal seller of the telephones themselves.

BUZZ BOX

Most telephones at home and at work now have an answering machine to record messages. The first answering machine in Britain was sold in 1958. It was called "Answering Machine No. 1".

THE EXPANSION OF TELEPHONES

In 1979, a new Conservative government was elected into office. They wanted to put state-controlled industries back into private hands. In 1984, British Telecom (or BT) was born as a private company. Since 1985, other companies such as Mercury and Vodaphone have started to provide telephone services in Britain. This created competition which helped to make telephone calls cheaper for everybody.

▶ A man tries out a "Trimphone" at Hampstead Town Hall, 1965.

▲ Two teenagers look at a text message. Most teenagers today own a mobile.

THE RISE OF THE MOBILE TELEPHONE

It was only in 1985 that the first mobile telephones arrived in Britain. They were very large (they were nicknamed "bricks"), very expensive and they only worked in London. In the next few years the rest of the country was covered by mobile telephone providers. As the size of mobile telephones shrank and costs fell, more and more people bought a mobile telephone. Today there are more mobile telephones than people in Britain. Texting became commonplace in the late 1990s. Today over four billion texts are sent every month in Britain.

▶ The BT "Telecom Tower" in London. It sends telephone, Internet and television signals around the world.

TIMELINE

1947
The General Post Office (GPO) is nationalised.

1956
The first telephone cable between Britain and North America is laid.

1958
The first answering machine is sold in Britain.

1984
The telephone service is privatised.

1985
The first mobile phones arrive in Britain.

1992
Texting from mobile phones becomes possible.

" The first mobile phone I had was provided by the company I worked for in 1983. It was a "Nokia Talkman 450 Mobira Senator". I say mobile phone but it was more like a modern day phone box. The technology has changed hugely since I had my first mobile phone. Now though if you don't have a mobile phone you're not a normal citizen. "

Tom, UK.

19

The personal computer has only existed for just over 30 years. In that time it has changed the lives of British people almost beyond recognition. Whether it is for entertainment, education or even shopping, the computer at home has had a huge effect on Britain since World War II.

THE FIRST HOME COMPUTERS

Nobody in Britain had a computer at home until 1974. In that year Atari released a computer that was designed to play simple computer games. Three years later Apple started selling the Apple II. This computer is seen as the very first computer for the home. However, it was very expensive and took a lot of skill to operate. In 1981, IBM created a computer for the home that used an operating system called MS-DOS. In 1985, this became the Windows operating system. As computers became cheaper and more powerful, more and more people began to use them at home.

THEN AND NOW

In 1948 there was only one computer in the whole of Britain. It was based at the University of Manchester and was called the "Manchester Baby". Today there are 10 million British households with a computer and an even larger number in our schools, offices and shops.

" I remember getting our first IBM PC around 1982. My most fond memory was hearing my mother exclaim how she could have re-carpeted the entire house for what we paid for it "

Marc Sternin remembering the high cost of the first IBM PCs.

◄ A man working on an IBM Personal Computer in 1986.

◄ Today most young people have access to the Internet and browse chatroooms and other sites from the World Wide Web.

TIMELINE

1948
Britain's first digital computer is built at the University of Manchester.

1977
Apple release the first proper home computer.

1981
IBM produce a personal computer with MS-DOS.

1985
The first Windows system released.

1993
The World Wide Web (www) is available in people's homes.

2004
Over half of all households in Britain have Internet access.

THE WORLD WIDE WEB

The first ever web pages were created in 1990. At first they were used by governments and large businesses. However, in 1993 web browsers began to appear and it became more popular for use in the home. Today over 90 per cent of households in Britain have access to the Internet at home.

CHANGING OUR LIVES

The personal computer has allowed us to communicate with each other faster and to give us new ways to learn and to have fun. However, there are fears that increased shopping on the internet will mean that our cities and towns will change as people use shops less and less. Some people are also concerned that social networking sites such as MySpace, Bebo and Facebox are making young people less part of their local community.

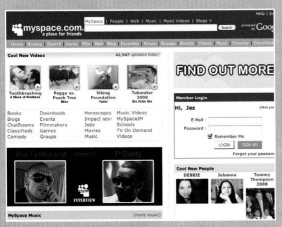

▲ The popular Myspace website, which attracts millions of visitors from all around the world today.

BUZZ BOX

The most popular website in Britain in 2006 was Zylom, a website with free online games. The most popular British website is the BBC website. Over 2 million people visit the BBC website every day.

Today, British people can listen to music in their homes in many different ways. Nearly every household has more than one CD player. Now people can download music from different websites and listen to them on an MP3 player. However, before the 1980s, British people mostly listened to music on vinyl records.

THE ALBUM AND THE SINGLE

During World War II, music in the home came from 78 rpm records. They had this name because the records turned on a turntable 78 times per minute. The music was recorded into grooves in the record. A needle picked up the recorded music which was amplified though a speaker. In the years after World War II, the 78 record was gradually replaced by the 33 and 45 rpm records. The 33 rpm record first arrived in Britain in 1948 and the 45 rpm record (below left) came a year later. 33 rpm records were 12 inches (30 cm) in diameter and 45 rpm records were 7 inches (18cm) in diameter. They became albums (or LPs) and singles respectively.

THE RISE OF THE RECORD

These new kinds of record arrived at the same time as the appearance of pop music in the USA. Pop groups such as Bill Haley and the Comets were able to sell one song on a single and a collection of songs on albums. In 1952, the singles chart began showing the best-selling singles every week.

BUZZ BOX

In 1965, the cassette was launched. It offered a recordable alternative to the LP. However in 2007 many British stores announced they were to stop selling cassettes, leaving customers with a choice of vinyl, CD and MP3 formats.

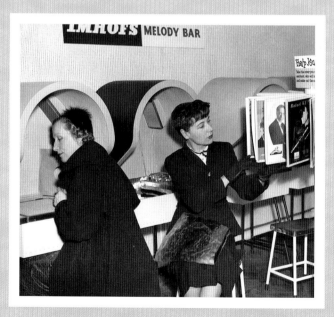

▲ A Melody Bar from 1953. Customers selected records and could listen to them in special booths.

> *When I got my iPod I put all of my CDs on it. Then I download music from an online store. Now I've run out of music to put on the thing and there's still space for more.*
>
> **Naomi Kitchen on recording music onto her iPod, 2007.**

▲ A cassette player. In 2007, many shops announced they were no longer selling cassettes.

NEW WAYS OF LISTENING TO MUSIC

The first portable format for listening to music was the cassette. They first arrived in Britain in 1965. However, the right machines for playing them (called "cassette decks") did not appear until the early 1970s. Most cassettes were sold as blanks and people would record music on to them. Music companies tried to stop this because it meant that they would lose money.

DIGITAL MUSIC

In 1983, a new way of listening to music arrived in Britain. The CD had been invented in Japan the year before and was seen as a way of recording and playing music. By 1988, sales of records and cassettes had been overtaken by CD sales. Today CDs are under threat from the arrival of the MP3 player. The first MP3 player arrived in Britain in 1999, but it was only with the arrival of the iPod in 2001 that it became a popular way of listening to music.

▶ An iPod Nano. This MP3 player is capable of storing 2,000 songs even though it is less than an inch thick.

1948
The 33 rpm, 12 inch (30 cm) record arrives in Britain. The 45 rpm, 7 inch (18 cm) record arrives in 1949.

1952
The first singles chart appears in Britain.

1965
The cassette is first sold in Britain.

1983
CDs appear.

1999
MP3s arrive in UK.

2001
Apple launch the iPod.

2005
The singles chart includes legally downloaded music.

THEN AND NOW

The 45 rpm 7 inch single record had two songs: one on each side of the record. Each song lasted about 3 to 4 minutes. Most MP3 players can store up to 1,000 songs. This is about 65 hours of music.

Before the end of World War II there was not really any such thing as "pop" music. In the 1940s, the most popular kinds of music were jazz, mostly played by American musicians like Duke Ellington and Louis Armstrong, and music hall acts like George Formby, Gracie Fields and Flanagan & Allen.

▲ Pop group The Beatles (from left: Paul McCartney, George Harrison, Ringo Starr and John Lennon) performing in 1963.

ROCK AND ROLL

The first pop music that appealed to just young people arrived in Britain in 1956 with the release of a film called *Blackboard Jungle*. On the film was a song by Bill Haley and the Comets called *Rock Around the Clock*. In the same year Elvis Presley released his first record in Britain. His stage act outraged many older people but teenagers loved him. Soon British acts like Cliff Richard and Billy Fury began to copy these acts.

THE BRITISH INVASION

The 1960s was the decade in which British pop music swept the world. At the front of this invasion was The Beatles. "Beatlemania" worried many people as thousands of screaming fans followed them wherever they went. In 1964, they went to the United States and "Beatlemania" arrived there as well. Other British bands, like the Rolling Stones, also had huge successes in the United States.

THE YEARS OF EXCESS

In the 1970s, British pop music changed. The songs became louder, the concerts more outrageous and "glam rock" and "heavy metal" were born. The top British bands were Led Zeppelin, The Sweet and Slade. However, in 1976, "punk rock" arrived and managed to upset

THEN AND NOW

When *Blackboard Jungle* was released in 1956, there was fighting in Liverpool between the police and young people who had been to see the film. Many people believed that the music in the film encouraged young people to be violent. In June 2006, the politician David Cameron accused Radio 1 of encouraging crime by playing hip-hop with violent lyrics on the Tim Westwood Show.

1952
The first British singles chart is launched.

1956
The release of the film "Blackboard Jungle".

Elvis Presley has his first hit in Britain.

1963
The Beatles have their first number one hit.

1964
The first "Top of the Pops" is broadcast.

1976
Punk rock comes to everybody's notice.

late 1980s
Boy bands and girl groups become very popular.

Hip-hop, rap and house music also appear.

2006
The last "Top of the Pops" is broadcast.

just about everybody. The Sex Pistols swore on daytime television, released singles and albums that were either banned by radio stations or shops refused to sell. Punk fashion with ripped leather jackets, safety pins as jewellery and spiky hair also alarmed some people.

▼ The hip-hop artist Kanye West performing in 2007. He is one of a number of rappers promoting a positive message through their music, rather than the stereotypical violent image associated with the genre.

NICE AND NASTY

British pop music since the 1980s has been dominated by the rise of the boy (and girl) bands and dance music like House, rap and hip-hop. The most famous boy bands have been Boyzone (formed in 1994), Take That (formed in 1991) and Westlife (formed in 1999). The songs that they sang were often harmonious love songs which appealed to a large number of people. In 1996, Britain's most successful girl group was formed – the Spice Girls. They had a record six number ones. Rap and hip-hop artists such as Eminem and Tupac Shakur were also very popular but, they were often criticised for singing songs said by some people to encourage violence.

BUZZ BOX

The artist with the most number one singles in Britain is Elvis Presley with 21 chart toppers. The top group is The Beatles with 17 number ones. The top woman singer is Madonna with 12 and the top girl group is the Spice Girls with six.

25

Many of the toys and games that modern children play with today would be familiar to a child from the 1940s. For instance, games like "Ludo" and "Monopoly" were all invented before World War II. However many toys and games, especially electronic and computer games, have appeared in the bedrooms of children since 1948, and have changed the way we choose to spend our leisure time.

▲ A family sit down for a game of "Scrabble" in 1959. Board games remain popular today despite the rise of games consoles.

NEW BOARD GAMES

Games and toy manufacturers are always on the lookout for new games to sell. Since World War II there have been several board games that have become very popular in Britain. In 1955, a new game arrived in Britain from the USA. It was called "Scrabble" and tested players' knowledge of words and it very quickly became a popular game with both adults and children. Another board game that needed some knowledge was "Trivial Pursuit". It came to Britain from Canada in 1981.

OUTDOOR GAMES

In the summer of 1971, the "Spacehopper" was launched. It was an orange vinyl toy you could sit and bounce about on. It had been invented in Italy three years before, and it instantly became a new craze. Other outdoor toys like skateboards arose in the 1950s, and are still very popular pastimes.

> 66 *I'm 43 and had a 'Spacehopper' when I was nine years old. My funniest memory is when my little brother, who was aged three at the time, and I were playing at a field near our house. I told him a bull was coming out of the field and was going to chase us. He jumped onto the 'Spacehopper', never looked back and bounced all the way back to our house* 99

Helen Craig remembering playing with a Spacehopper in the early 1970s.

▲ A teenage boy skateboarding at a recreation ground in Harrow.

Many toys are linked to television programmes. The Dr Who games appeared in 1965. Toy Daleks were the most popular. In 2006, a Cyberman mask was voted "Toy of the Year" by Britain's toy shops.

early 1950s
Skateboarding starts in America and soon moves to Britain.

1971
British children start bouncing on "Spacehoppers".

1975
The first home computer game, "Pong", goes on sale.

1980
The "Rubik's Cube" arrives in Britain.

1984
The computer game "Pacman" is launched.

1996
"Pokemon" comes to Britain from Japan.

2004
"Robosapian", the first successful robot toy, arrives in Britain.

▼ In 2007 Nintendo launched the Wii console. It had a remote device which was used to play sports games, for example, in the same way you would play the real game. You swing the controls to hit a the ball in the baseball game, for example.

COMPUTER GAMES

The first computer game that could be played at home arrived in Britain in 1975. It was called "Pong" and was a simple tennis game. Computer games became much more popular with a character called Mario who appeared in a game called "Donkey Kong". He soon appeared in games by himself. "Sonic the Hedgehog" first came to computer screens in 1991. Since then computer games have become more sophisticated and the number of games consoles has grown. Some people are concerned that children are spending too much time playing computer games and that games like "Grand Theft Auto" are far too violent and could make players more aggressive.

BUZZ BOX

Sometimes toys are seen as so dangerous that they have been banned. In 2003, a fluid-filled ball on a string called the Yucky Yo Ball became very popular amongst British children. It was soon banned by the British government because of safety fears.

GLOSSARY

Broadsheet	A newspaper that uses larger size paper.
CD (Compact Disc)	A small plastic disc on which music can be recorded.
Commercial stations	Radio and television stations who use advertising to pay for their programmes.
Daily newspaper	A newspaper that appears every day except Sunday.
Games console	Special hardware for playing computer games.
Fringe theatre	Plays that are not part of the "mainstream". They normally tackle difficult subjects and are performed at small theatres.
Home computer	Another phrase for a personal computer.
Internet	The Internet is a way of linking together computers all over the world so that they can exchange information.
ITV	ITV stands for Independent Television. Britain's largest commercial television company.
"Kitchen-sink" drama	A kind of play that was popular in the 1950s. The phrase refers to the play being about ordinary people in ordinary homes.
MP3	A digital music file that can be played on a MP3 player.
Multiplex	A cinema with a lot of screens showing different films.
Nationalised	When an industry is taken out of private hands and is owned by the government.
Operating system	A computer program that manages other pieces of software. Windows and Linus are examples.
PCs	Personal computers. These are normally computers for use in the home.
Pirate radio station	Radio stations that broadcast illegally.
Privatization	When a government-owned company is sold into private hands.
Records	A vinyl disc on which music is recorded.
South Bank	An area on the south side of the River Thames which hosted the Festival of Britain and now has a variety of theatres, cinemas and concert halls.
Tabloid	A newspaper that uses smaller size paper.
Who-dunnit	A murder mystery play. *The Mousetrap* is one example.

WEBLINKS

http://www.htw.info/
A website that explores the history of television in Britain.

http://www.museumoflondon.org.uk/archive/exhibits/festival/index.htm
A website from the Museum of London that explores the Festival of Britain.

http://www.connected-earth.com/
This website from BT looks at the history of communication in Britain.

http://www.britishtheatreguide.info/articles/300100a.htm
A guide to the history of British theatre since World War II.

http://www.televisionheaven.co.uk/kids.htm
A website that takes an affectionate look at the most popular children's television programmes.

http://inventors.about.com/library/inventors/blcomputer_videogames.htm
A website all about the history of computer games.

http://www.bfi.org.uk/education/
A website from the British Film Institute with a lot of materials on British film and cinemas.

http://www.vam.ac.uk/moc/
The website of the Museum of Childhood in London. It contains information on how children have lived their lives during the 20th century.

Note to parents and teachers: Every effort has been made by the Publishers to ensure that these websites are suitable for children, that they are of the highest educational value, and that they contain no inappropriate or offensive material. However, because of the nature of the Internet, it is impossible to guarantee that the contents of these sites will not be altered. We strongly advise that Internet access is supervised by a responsible adult.

INDEX